GETTING A JOB IN
BUILDING
MAINTENANCE

PHILIP WOLNY

ROSEN
PUBLISHING®

NEW YORK

For my father, Mike Hetlof

Published in 2014 by The Rosen Publishing Group, Inc.
29 East 21st Street, New York, NY 10010

First Edition

Library of Congress Cataloging-in-Publication Data

Wolny, Philip.
Getting a job in building maintenance/Philip Wolny.—
1st ed.—New York: Rosen, © 2014
        p. cm.—(Job basics: getting the job you need)
Includes bibliographical references and index.
ISBN 978-1-4488-9608-0
1. Buildings—Maintenance—Vocational guidance—Juvenile literature.
2. Repairing trades—Vocational guidance—Juvenile literature. 3. Building trades—Vocational guidance—Juvenile literature. 3. Building—Vocational guidance—United States. I. Title.
HD8039.R469 .W65 2014
331.702'0835

Manufactured in the United States of America

CPSIA Compliance Information: Batch #S13YA: For further information, contact Rosen Publishing, New York, New York, at 1-800-237-9932.

CONTENTS

INTRODUCTION

It is 8:50 on a Monday morning. A young man enters the lobby of an apartment building, anxious but excited for his first day of work. His boss, the building manager, starts him out with a tour of the building. It is a five-story building with about forty apartments, or units. There is much to learn and get acquainted with.

In the back office, the young man changes from his street clothes into a crisp, new uniform. The building manager shows him the trash compactor, boiler, alarm and safety systems, the laundry room's washers and dryers, and other machinery and equipment that he will help run and maintain. In the process, they run into some of the building's tenants, and the new worker politely introduces himself. A delivery person drops off a month's supply of water, and the young man signs for it and helps load the large water cooler bottles into a storage space. His tour of the building continues as he is shown a list of outstanding work requests for various tenants. One apartment needs a new doorknob installed, for example, while another has a leaky kitchen faucet.

It might seem a bit overwhelming, but the new recruit is ready for it, recalling the various classes he took as part of his course work at a vocational training school. His skills in heating, ventilation, and air-conditioning (HVAC) are particularly strong. But he may need some additional practice with painting and lawn care. With a valuable internship under his belt

Building maintenance is an exciting, challenging, and productive career path. It is a great choice for those who are good at and enjoy working with their hands. Customer service, the ability to learn new things, and teamwork all go with the territory.

and some certifications, he is confident he can do well at this new job.

Getting a job in building maintenance is a great career choice, especially for young people who like to work with their hands. Working in this field can mean having many different job titles: building maintenance technician, superintendent, property manager, and many more. It is also a wise path because building maintenance workers will always be in demand. They are crucial to making sure that everyone else can live, work, and play (in the case of gyms, theaters, and stadiums) comfortably and safely.

Think about the everyday things that we all take for granted. These range from having the electricity necessary to power our homes and offices and computers, to having easy access to clean and properly working bathrooms, to staying warm in the winter and cool in the summer. It is really only when these things fail in some way that people truly appreciate the work of building maintenance staff.

This career requires technical skills, problem-solving abilities, and being good with people. Getting a start requires getting the proper education and certifications, patience, and hard work. It is a step-by-step process that someone can begin years before entering the job market. Being professional, making good contacts, doing well in course work, and being efficient and active in one's job search will eventually lead to a good job in building maintenance.

The Inner Workings of a Career in Building Maintenance

Building maintenance workers perform many different kinds of physical work. They work on and within various types of buildings. These can include apartment and office buildings, schools, retail stores, factories, hospitals, hotels, stadiums and arenas, and more. They receive training to handle a wide range of maintenance and repair jobs, rather than concentrating on just one specialized task.

Building maintenance workers are often skilled in many basic types of physical and technical labor. They might fix and replace plumbing, paint interior and exterior walls, handle electrical wiring, replace broken glass, fix doors, lay tiles, clean hallways, and collect and dispose of trash and waste. Sometimes this all occurs in a single day! Other duties often include fixing locks; maintaining and running boilers, heating, ventilation, air-conditioning and other cooling systems; unclogging drains and fixing other plumbing; general carpentry; and much more.

Workers in this field not only handle the smooth operation of a building's inner workings. They must also deal with

The building maintenance field offers employees the chance to work in many different kinds of facilities. Here, Rodney Pahneena vacuums Caccia Field, part of the Holt Arena, in Pocatello, Idaho. This is the home of the Idaho State University Bengals football team.

issues like roof, exterior wall, and fence maintenance and repair. If a building has a yard, a lawn, hedges, or other greenery, building maintenance technicians may be in charge of taking care of these as well.

Another important duty is handling paperwork and other nonphysical duties that aid in building repair and maintenance. Someone needs to schedule and track appointments with outside contractors. These include carpenters, electricians, and other specialists who are often needed for more complex maintenance, repair, and installation jobs. Building maintenance workers may also order necessary items, like cleaning products, tools, replacement machine parts, and any other supplies necessary for the upkeep and smooth functioning of a building.

Workers will also arrange for important health and safety checkups, including inspections of elevators, boilers, and other important equipment. This may also entail maintaining and replacing safety equipment like smoke and carbon monoxide detectors, sprinkler systems, and fire and safety alarms.

Be a Jack of All Trades

Building maintenance is a great career choice for someone who is handy. Unlike specialists in particular trades (like carpenters, electricians, or plumbers), building maintenance managers need to know a little bit of everything. Their training programs include classes in many different types of mechanical and electrical repair and maintenance. Later, they build and expand upon these skills with on-the-job training.

For this reason, young people thinking about a future job in building maintenance need not worry about having extensive training in any one skill or specialization. They should feel confident in having a general and basic grasp of mechanics, electronics, electrical repair, and other traditional handyman skills. Most jobs, even entry-level ones, require completion of a degree from a building maintenance program or similar technical training, internships, or apprenticeships.

Types of Workplace

Employment options in building maintenance differ according to the size and type of workplace. A sports stadium or entertainment complex may employ dozens of workers. Hotels, hospitals, schools, government buildings, movie theaters, shopping malls, and other large workplaces also have large maintenance staffs. In some cases, a larger staff will require

BUILDING MAINTENANCE: DO YOU HAVE WHAT IT TAKES?

Building maintenance means many different things, but successful workers in the field will generally have the following qualities:

- Be willing to get their hands dirty, literally, because their duties will include cleaning, painting, mechanical repair, and more.
- Be physically fit and in good health. Workers may have to walk, kneel, crouch, climb, and carry heavy things, like boxes, equipment, and tools.
- Be computer literate and math-savvy because modern maintenance is becoming ever more automated, digitized, and electronic in nature.
- Be good with people. Many of their tasks bring building maintenance workers in close contact with residents, tenants, guests, visitors, coworkers, and contractors.
- Be versatile and quick learners. A "jack of all trades" is a perfect candidate for building maintenance.

certain workers who specialize in a particular type of work. One employee may handle HVAC, for example, while others will concentrate on electrical work, plumbing, landscaping, or general upkeep.

A small apartment building typically employs a single superintendent—a "super"—who handles the tenants' and building's needs. He or she may live nearby or often live rent-free in the building itself while also collecting a modest salary. For more complicated or specialized repairs, the super will contact and coordinate the efforts of outside contractors. The lone super must be comfortable with and capable of a wide variety of building maintenance work.

Plumbing Systems

Building maintenance technicians will usually be responsible for a property's plumbing system. A building's public bathroom facilities include sinks, toilets, urinals, and hand dryers, while residential bathrooms contain showers and/or bathtubs. Apartment buildings and hotels will also include laundry rooms with numerous washing machines. Apartments often also feature dishwashers in each unit. A super, custodian, or other maintenance worker will replace or fix pipes, bath fixtures, and toilet mechanisms; lay out or replace bathroom tile; and perform routine maintenance on the plumbing system and individual appliances and fixtures.

Plumbing is one of many potential responsibilities for building maintenance workers. It is one of the ways that they work behind the scenes to help tenants use their residences and workplaces smoothly and efficiently. Here, a maintenance worker inspects the pipes under a sink.

At times, maintenance workers will also fix or replace pipes that deliver clean water and remove wastewater. Getting to these pipes to fix a problem involves demolishing walls or floors with crowbars and other tools. After the repair has been made, a worker must then patch up the holes by plastering, painting, and/or retiling.

Light and Power

Offices, apartments, theaters, stadiums, shopping centers, and other facilities need electrical power to ensure that everything runs smoothly, including electronics, appliances, computers, and HVAC systems. Building maintenance workers must make sure the electrical system and everything it powers are working properly.

Maintenance duties might be as simple as replacing lightbulbs and fluorescent lights in apartments, offices, or hallways. They may also include more complex tasks like fixing damaged electrical outlets; installing wire for electrical circuits, as well as circuit breakers and fuses; measuring electrical flow or voltage; and reading and interpreting the blueprints of a building's electrical grid.

Heating and Cooling

Buildings need to be warmed in cold weather and cooled in warm weather. Building maintenance workers may need to install, repair, or maintain heating systems, which may be run using electricity, gas, or oil. These may include water-based heating systems that keep building occupants warm and provide them with hot water. Often, the same system is used to cool a building if it has central air-conditioning, rather than individual window units. In larger buildings, these networks may be very complex and must be checked regularly to replace parts that have worn down. They must also be inspected to prevent buildup of dangerous substances like mold or debris that might become a fire hazard.

Troubleshooting Complex Systems

The technology used in the construction and maintenance of buildings has improved greatly in the last two decades. Systems that control all aspects of a building's operations have become more complex and automated. This means that they are controlled electronically, often with the aid of computer systems.

Energy management systems, for example, monitor and control all aspects of many newer, larger buildings and complexes. Building maintenance professionals are being trained in school and on the job to operate these complicated systems. Given how advanced the power plants and operating systems of newer buildings are getting, maintenance workers must expect to do more than simply minor repairs and upkeep as they advance through their careers.

Some people have a common misconception of building maintenance workers. They often imagine a group of people sitting around in a boiler room, eating sandwiches, playing cards, and waiting to hear and respond to resident and client complaints. In reality, much of a maintenance worker's job is to prevent problems from occurring. They don't have time to sit and wait for a problem to occur. Instead they are always busy maintaining the building, its systems, and its fixtures and

Building maintenance technicians must be comfortable with both new technologies and traditional ones, along with using specialized tools. Terry Moxley cuts the heat stack of a boiler to be removed in a school in Augusta, Georgia.

appliances in order to prevent any large-scale breakdowns or malfunctions. They approach their work site as preventative problem solvers and troubleshooters with ever-growing technical expertise.

Maintenance workers must be competent and flexible, able to work with both older mechanical systems and newer, digital ones. Above all, they must be able to grow in and adapt to a changing workplace and career field.

Managing Wear and Tear

Occupants and other clients often request new equipment or repairs. Refrigerators, ovens, dishwashers, washing machines and dryers, and other appliances are among the items that must be periodically serviced or replaced. Doors and windows suffer damage from normal daily use. Systems that seem to be working just fine must nevertheless be constantly inspected, maintained, and serviced to prevent major breakdowns. In building maintenance, the old saying applies: "An ounce of prevention is worth a pound of cure."

Interiors and Exteriors

Building maintenance workers are often also responsible for keeping the interiors and exteriors of buildings clean and tidy. Cleaning involves mopping floors, shampooing carpets, vacuuming, window washing, dusting, and other tasks.

Every facility or building requires maintenance both inside and outside. Alvin Parker, a maintenance man employed at Hyde Park Union Church in Chicago, Illinois, gathers fallen leaves outside the church.

Maintenance workers must also clean building exteriors, including the disposing of fallen leaves and the shoveling of snow from the driveways, entrances, and sidewalks that surround a property. Workers must clean and maintain rooftops and building siding to prevent leaks, holes, and other structural damage that can let the weather get into a building and lead to flooding, moisture, or mold problems.

Another major job is the proper disposal of waste and garbage. Garbage may need to be collected and disposed of by building staff or dropped down a chute to a garbage compactor, which must be run regularly and emptied. Workers also may need to ensure that occupants are properly separating recyclable materials like glass, plastic, metal, and paper waste. In some buildings, maintenance workers do the separation themselves.

Inspections and Safety

An important aspect of a building maintenance worker's job is to help ensure the health and safety of the building's occupants and visitors. To do this, he or she must make sure that safety inspectors visit regularly to check that elevators and other equipment are working properly. Environmental inspections are also needed to identify and fix any gas leaks and prevent the spread of mold, which can threaten occupants' health and the building's structure. In the coming years, many more buildings will be required to meet "green" certification standards. These standards help guarantee that a building is meeting all local, state, and federal environmental standards, including goals for energy efficiency, waste reduction and disposal, toxins, air quality, and recycling.

City, state, and federal inspectors often perform inspections to make sure property owners are complying with all the relevant environmental laws. Maintenance workers must make sure the building meets all the necessary codes. If anything is found to be lacking, they must make the appropriate fixes to get the building back into compliance with the law.

Building maintenance workers regularly perform their own inspections of the premises in order to make sure that nothing is breaking or degrading and posing a danger to others. They also handle minor security issues, like quickly replacing broken doors, locks, windows, and security systems to make sure criminals or other intruders do not enter.

Management and Supervision

Larger buildings and complexes will often have correspondingly large staffs. A sports complex, for instance, may employ dozens of workers. Higher-level managers—sometimes called property, site, or building managers—oversee the work of other maintenance staff and handle the hiring and firing of personnel.

Maintenance workers often start at the bottom and work their way up the ladder over the years, eventually reaching the level of management. They expand their skills by gaining experience on the job and by continuing their formal and practical education. In large organizations, employees on a career track even receive training on more complicated and higher-level aspects of building maintenance, like project or staff management.

The higher up the ladder maintenance workers go, the more money they earn. However, their responsibilities

A building maintenance worker trudges through a flooded basement in the Knickerbocker Village Houses after Hurricane Irene hit New York City. Such workers are often on the front lines of cleaning up and ensuring building safety in the wake of such disasters.

naturally increase, too. Managers may need to respond quickly to situations that cannot wait until the next day's business hours. A pipe that bursts and begins flooding a basement, a downed tree during a thunderstorm, or an emergency request from a tenant or occupant must be addressed at that moment, not at 9 o'clock the next morning. A manager might even be called into work on a day off or in the middle of the night to deal with problems and emergencies. Building managers are ultimately responsible for both the good and the bad work performed by their subordinates. Managers are the ones who must answer to tenants and owners for all maintenance work performed in the building.

School's In: Educational Opportunities

The road to a building maintenance career can begin early. Handy teenagers can help out parents with minor home repairs or tinker with appliances, bikes, or even the family car. As they get older, teens can transform their hobbies into concrete and useful skills.

Vocational Education

Training high school students in technical skills that prepare them for specific jobs, or vocations, is known as vocational education. For much of the twentieth century, vocational-technical (or "vo-tech") programs included classes such as wood and metal shop, drafting, automotive repair, typing and business courses, and home economics. Though they are less common now, many schools continue to offer shop classes as electives. Metal and wood shop, where teens learn the basics of metalworking and carpentry, are great classes for those who enjoy working with their hands.

Handy teens interested in building maintenance careers can benefit greatly from attending a vocational-technical high school. In some places, this type of high school training is

Vocational training in high school remains an invaluable resource for youth hoping to break into building maintenance. William Logan *(left)*, a wood shop teacher at Jordan High School in the Watts district of Los Angeles, California, helps Bobby Kimbrough cut wood during class.

known as career and technical education (CTE). Some high schools offer vo-tech programs in conjunction with local community colleges.

Career Training and College Credit

Many vocational high schools, and even traditional ones, offer teens the possibility of getting technical career training while also receiving college credits. These college credits can then be applied to programs the students may enter in two- or four-year colleges or specialized technical schools. High school career or guidance counselors often have information about these opportunities.

Vo-tech programs are sometimes run with the cooperation of local technical schools and community colleges. These programs often offer courses in construction and building maintenance occupations, including residential and commercial building maintenance and remodeling, plumbing, electrical systems, refrigeration, and HVAC.

The benefit of such courses, and of vocational high schools in general, is that teens gain hands-on experience. They use tools, read technical manuals and blueprints, and work with modern equipment and facilities provided by both their own schools and participating educational institutions. Federal and state government programs fund these programs. This money helps schools acquire the most modern equipment and provide the most up-to-date information on current and cutting-edge building technology.

Apprenticeships

Most apprenticeships in skilled manual labor are offered for specific types of tradespeople (like carpenters, electricians, welders, etc.). Yet one can also apply for apprenticeships specifically in building maintenance. An apprenticeship is a job opportunity in which someone learns under more qualified and experienced individuals while still earning money. An apprentice usually makes a lower wage at the beginning, which increases slowly as training continues. Becoming an apprentice means committing the same time and effort one would to a traditional full-time job. During the course of an apprenticeship, which can last for several years, one might need to put in several thousand hours of labor and a few hundred hours of classroom work.

Advantages of an apprenticeship including "getting one's hands dirty" right away. Apprentices also lend themselves to the development of good professional contacts and job placement opportunities, often with the same employer or organization with whom they were done. Some apprenticeships last only a couple of years, while others last as long as five or six.

Trade organizations and labor unions interested in ensuring there will be qualified workers in the future for specific industries often sponsor apprenticeship programs. Nonprofit

Apprenticeships offer great experience and training. Cedar Rapids, Iowa, residents Nick Peiffer *(left)* and Scott Adair work with sheet metal during an apprenticeship program. Apprentices in this program require four years of evening classes, two nights a week, ten months of the year.

organizations and local, state, and federal government departments and agencies also support them. Many offer apprenticeship opportunities to youths who have just completed or are about to complete high school.

Mentors

Another way to break into building maintenance is to seek out a mentor—an older, experienced worker who has long been employed in the field and has a lot of experience, expertise, and inside information and tips to share with you. Mentors can also let you know about any job openings they are aware of and can even recommend you for a job.

Teens seek mentors to help train and advise them in exchange for helping out as assistants or employees. This can be a more informal alternative to an apprenticeship. Even if the work they do under a mentor is not directly related to building maintenance, the skills involved can improve their future education, job prospects, and professional contacts in the field.

Community Colleges and Trade and Technical Schools

Many community colleges nationwide offer two-year associate's degree programs in fields related to building maintenance. These are usually an Associate of Science, or A.S., degree. The names of such programs vary. They are often referred to as building maintenance technology or facilities maintenance technology programs.

COURSE SELECTIONS

A sampling of classes from the Facilities Maintenance Technology program at the Community College of Allegheny County, PA:

FIRST SEMESTER: Basic Electrical Wiring; Heating Systems; Air-Conditioning Systems

SECOND SEMESTER: Job Safety and First Aid; Plumbing Maintenance; Brazing and Welding

THIRD SEMESTER: English Composition 1; Mathematics for the Industries; Oral Communication

FOURTH SEMESTER: English Composition 2 or Technical Communications; Physical Science for the Industries; Introduction to Psychology or Organizational Psychology

SAMPLING OF ELECTIVES: Blueprint Reading; Duct and Hydronic System Design; Plumbing Skills 1; Electrical Motor Control; Fluid Power Systems; HVAC Installation; Industry Competency Exam preparation

Students who want to enter the workforce more quickly can complete a certificate degree instead of an A.S. Certificate degrees qualify the student for entry-level positions in the field. The advantage of studying longer and gaining an A.S. degree is that those students develop more advanced skills and can apply for and obtain higher-paying positions upon graduation.

The most common road to working in building maintenance is to attend a trade or technical school. While community colleges offer technical training alongside a wide variety of other subjects, trade and technical schools specialize exclusively in the skilled manual trades. Trade schools are mostly private, for-profit businesses.

Guidance or career counselors can help students make decisions on coursework, training, which college or technical school to attend after graduation, and how to navigate the process of obtaining financial aid. Here, a guidance counselor helps a student sort through his options.

Student Loans and Financial Aid

Figuring out how to pay for school is another important step for anyone interested in pursuing the necessary education and training for a career in building maintenance. Nowadays, student loan debt has become a huge problem for many people in the workforce, even those who graduated decades ago and now have well-paying and stable jobs.

Visiting a high school guidance or career counselor is one way to start researching financial aid options. Counselors will have information on federal and state financial aid programs, scholarships, and other paths to help pay for your education and training. High schools, especially technical high schools, may offer industry-related scholarships. Good or excellent grades are necessary, as well as the fulfilling of certain application requirements, such as a personal essay and rec-ommendations from teachers and employers.

In addition, most colleges and trade schools, especially private technical schools, will have staff available to meet with curious students. Applicants should go prepared to ask as many questions as possible about the aid options available.

There are several types of financial aid available to those pursuing building maintenance careers, and most students use a combination of them. Accredited schools may offer their own financial aid packages.

Scholarships

A scholarship is a financial grant offered by a school, non-profit organization, or other entity. It is awarded based on academic merit. This means that it is given to students who get excellent grades. The student's financial need may also be taken into consideration when awarding a scholar-ship. Scholarship money does not need to be paid back, but the recipient usually has to maintain certain minimum grade levels.

High schools offer scholarships to graduating seniors, with money provided by individuals, companies, or other local institutions, such as trade or business associations and cor-porations. For example, Home Depot offers hundreds of scholarships a year for students entering the construction and building trades. Other parties that provide scholarships include fraternal, civic, religious, and community organiza-tions, as well as city, state, and federal agencies.

Loans and Grants

Federal government aid is also available in the form of loans and grants. Loans must be repaid, but not grants. Any student can download or pick up the Free Application for Federal Student Aid (FAFSA), fill it out, and work with a college or trade or technical school to figure out what type of aid he or she qualifies for. Federal Pell Grants are available for low-income students interested in vocational schools. Other government-funded loans include Stafford and Perkins loans, which have lower interest rates than private loans.

Students can also get student loans from private entities, like banks or loan lenders. The biggest loan lender is a financial services company called Sallie Mae that specializes in education funding. Private loans are more expensive in the long run because the percentage of the loan amount that must be paid back yearly, called the interest rate, is often higher than the interest rate on government student loans. Interest on private student loans can sometimes be extremely high.

Students should consider their options carefully. Many young borrowers carry heavy debt for years because they do not check the fine print on loans. Always consult parents or other responsible and knowledgeable adults, including school counselors, on the advantages and drawbacks of any loans, public or private. You should also research any company or organization you hope to borrow from. Scam artists frequently prey on uninformed young people. Even legitimate businesses employ predatory lending practices. They seem to go out of their way not to inform borrowers about the true long-term costs of a loan. Remember: if it seems too good to be true, it probably is.

Avoiding Fraud: Beware of Diploma Mills!

Doing the proper research before enrolling anywhere is key, especially when considering private, for-profit technical schools. One danger is attending a "diploma mill." Diploma mills are schools that promise to teach job skills and take students' money, but generally leave their paying students unqualified and unprepared to enter the workforce. Their teachers may be underqualified and the course work may be substandard.

Another way that diploma mills cheat students is by promising to place them in apprenticeships, internships, or paying jobs. Students later find that they receive little or no help in finding and obtaining these promised opportunities. Even if they get job interviews, applicants may be shocked to find out that employers do not want to hire them because of their school's bad reputation. Even those who do get a job often find that they are poorly prepared for the actual work of building maintenance and lack the basic know-how to be competent in their field.

Attendees listen to speaker Erika Heeb during the Cash for College event at the Los Angeles Convention Center. The convention is held by the California Student Aid Commission to assist low-income students with financial aid and college preparation.

Getting the Lowdown

Students should make sure all programs they apply for are properly accredited. Accreditation means that organizations and agencies have investigated and observed the school in question, its coursework, its faculty, and its students' post-graduation workplace preparedness. Accreditation is granted to schools that deliver quality education. The Council for Higher Education Accreditation (CHEA), the U.S. Department of Education (USDE), and the Council on Occupational Education (COE) are some of the most prominent entities that assist students in researching potential schools. They do so by offering detailed evaluations of the schools' quality and effectiveness.

Another helpful destination for anyone researching schools and colleges is the regional or state Web site for the Better Business Bureau (BBB). This is a national organization that tracks good and bad businesses and their practices. Schools with bad reputations can often be avoided by doing a simple Internet search or by contacting the above-mentioned organizations by phone, mail, or e-mail.

CHAPTER THREE

Pounding the Pavement: The Job Search

After school, what is the next step along the path that leads to a career in building maintenance? The actual job search is the next challenge. A successful job search can combine online job hunting, word-of-mouth leads and recommendations, and good old-fashioned pounding the pavement in one's town or city. Looking for work is often a mixture of hard work, persistence, determination, connections, and luck.

Internet-Based Job Searches

One of the first steps in the job search is going online. Nowadays, the Internet is one of the most efficient and convenient employment tools imaginable. It is quicker, easier, cheaper, and more comprehensive than shuffling through newspaper classified ads. It also allows users to narrow down their choices efficiently. Almost every company or employer out there has some kind of presence online. The important thing is to know where, and how, to look.

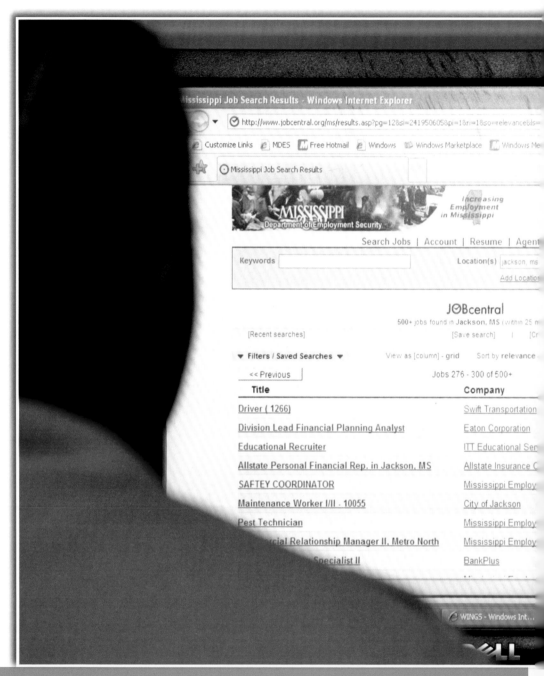

Using every resource available is a surefire way to maximize one's employment chances. Here, Corey Perry of Jackson, Mississippi, performs an online search using the JobCentral national employment network in his town's employment center.

Employment Web Sites

The largest online job sites include aggregator sites. Along with direct employer postings, these sites collect job listings from other Web sites and search engines from all across the Web. Some of the more popular job sites include Indeed, Monster, CareerBuilder, Simply Hired, Snagajob, AOL Jobs, Dice, JobBankUSA, and EmploymentGuide.

Among the most useful features of Internet-based job searches is the ability to plug in location-based data, such as town, state, or ZIP code, to find job openings near you. You may also be able to search for jobs by inputting other criteria, such as job title, location, desired salary, and type of work. You can also click on "Advanced Search" to further narrow down the results.

Using Keyword Searches

Keyword searches are crucial to an Internet-based job search. Sites will often allow for searching exact phrases in a job title or description, as well as more general keywords and phrases. Teens looking for building maintenance work can use some of the following search terms: "building maintenance," "building maintenance technician," "equipment," "repair," "building," "superintendent," "handy," "electrical," "plumbing," "HVAC," "property manager," "general contractor," "minor construction," and many more.

Uploading Résumés Online

Many employment Web sites allow users to upload résumés. First you must fill out some standard identifying information and create an account with a username and password. Once it is uploaded, the résumé is searchable by possible employers. These Web sites offer a related feature that sends out automated e-mails to you whenever a new job listing is posted that contains keywords that also appear in your résumé or were contained in previous job listings that you viewed or responded to.

Using School and Public Library Resources

Nearly every high school, community college, or technical school should have at least one person to consult about employment. In larger institutions, there is usually an office or employment center with a few counselors or other school employees to help job seekers. Teens should exploit these resources as often as they can.

Though many families and individuals have home computers, laptops, and even smartphones, this is not true for everyone. Luckily, schools, community centers, and other institutions often make computers available to students and the general public. Many such public computer labs also have office software installed, especially word processing programs for writing or retooling résumés.

Barring that, local libraries often have public computers. Usually, the only requirement is that users obtain a library card, often provided free of charge. Be aware, however, that,

Telephone Skills
Getting & Giving the Right Message

How to Choose a Career
A Guide to Self-Assessment

Making Contacts
Networking to Get Working

Job Leads
Who Can Help You Find a Job?

A job seeker, pictured in the background, searches for employment opportunities online at the Oakland Career Center in Oakland, California. In the foreground, printed materials offer job seekers important advice concerning networking, job search strategies, career options, and personal presentation.

depending on demand, there may be time limits on how long users can surf the Internet or use office software.

Another possible destination, if it is close enough, is a local branch office of the state department of labor. These offices will often have their computer labs specially desig-nated for job seekers. In addition to computers that can be used for online job searches and résumé building, each state's department of labor and employment also offers additional resources to help the unemployed and those just entering the workforce. These resources include informa-tion on special training courses, certification programs, apprenticeships, and internships.

A TIP ON RÉSUMÉ KEYWORDS

Keeping in mind that a one-page résumé is ideal, job applicants should include eye-catching keywords, while at the same time not going overboard. Stick to the "KISS Principle": "Keep It Short and Simple!" This means carefully reviewing job listings and including all the important keywords that appear in them in your résumé, but only if they actually apply to the training and experience you have.

When applying for positions with corporations or larger companies, candidates may compete with hundreds or even thousands of other applicants. Computer programs called applicant tracking systems (ATS) scan large numbers of résumés to help human resources departments narrow down the résumés to a far smaller collection that best match the company's needs and requirements. The computer programs scan résumés for certain important keywords, the very ones that appear in the job listing itself. The closer your résumé matches these, the more likely that it will be culled from the herd and you will be called in for an interview.

Trade and industry journals, both online and print editions, are another source of information for job seekers. Online editions of these journals occasionally host their own job boards. Hard copies of publications that do not offer free and open access to their online editions may be found at the library. By reading them, you can discover how an industry works, learn about the latest trends, and spark more job-hunting ideas.

Cold Calls and E-mails

Sending out dozens of résumés and cover letters can be a lot of work. Yet all that effort still may not yield an e-mail reply or call back, especially in a tough job market. Using the Internet, library, classifieds, and other information sources, teens can look up the addresses, e-mails, and phone numbers of employers who may not currently have public job postings. They can contact hotel chains, hospitals, sports complexes, manufacturing companies and factories, residential building management companies, retail chains, and many other types of employers. They can then simply ask if they are hiring currently or will be doing so in the near future.

By phone or via e-mail, teens should be straightforward and clear that they are looking for work. E-mails should have résumés attached. They should politely inquire to whom they should direct further inquiries and a résumé. Whenever possible, it is best to directly contact a person working in human resources.

If the person answering is friendly, it is recommended that you follow up periodically, perhaps once or twice a month, just to check in. When a job does become available, human resources will be more likely to remember and contact you. They may even do so before posting a job listing publicly.

Networking

There's an old saying: "It's not what you know, but who you know." What you know is obviously important, but networking with people one knows to find out about job openings is one of the best ways to get hired. Teens should consider any member of their own social networks as a potential source of employment information and recommendations: siblings, parents, other relatives, friends, family friends, neighbors, church and community members, teachers, guidance counselors and academic advisors, and former employers.

E-mail your contacts individually every once in a while, and remain friendly with former bosses, instructors, and others with industry connections. Teens who network have a better chance of hearing about jobs even before they are advertised to the general public. Employers routinely receive hundreds of résumés for every open job. Candidates known or recommended to them will have a better chance than strangers with otherwise similar backgrounds and experience.

Teens should also network with classmates, former coworkers, and people they meet through their hobbies and social interests. If you belong to a community organization,

Workforce development specialist Liz Kilkern *(right)* helps Vanessa Williams at the St. Louis Agency on Training & Employment, in St. Louis, Missouri. In addition to tapping personal and professional contacts, a smart job seeker will enlist the aid of government resources, too.

church, bicycling club, cooking class, or any other group that meets regularly, ask fellow members if they know of any job openings in your field.

Finally, joining a social network specifically geared toward employment and networking, such as the popular site LinkedIn, should be a main pillar of any teen's job-seeking strategy.

Doing the Legwork

Getting out into the real world to look for work is another necessary component of any job search. When doing so, dress professionally. This means wearing a suit and tie or business casual (a button-down shirt, khakis or skirt, and dress shoes, rather than sneakers), and visiting potential employers.

Physically explore your town or city, and keep an eye out for "Help Wanted" signs. Smaller employers, such as the property owners of a small apartment building, may not have much of an online presence, if any. They may also not have the resources or the time to hire employment agencies to interview and screen potential employees. The "Help Wanted" sign might be their only form of advertising.

Also visit businesses and sites that do not have signs up. Ask the person at the reception desk or the building manager if it is OK to leave a résumé. Also request any relevant application forms, specifying that you are seeking a building maintenance job (rather than a retail or service-oriented position). Politely ask whether there is anyone in particular who can be contacted, such as a building or facilities manager, to make further job inquiries. In the best-case scenario, a job seeker will be lucky enough to speak with that person on site and place a résumé directly into his or her hands.

A newly constructed building is one sign that building maintenance positions may be available soon. Looking around one's town or region, as well as scanning through local media, can provide valuable clues about where to most effectively target a job search.

Employees or managers can sometimes be unresponsive or cold, but not always. Being professional, friendly, and polite can go a long way toward winning over strangers. If a teen is fortunate enough to speak with a hiring manager, even briefly, that direct interpersonal contact can leave a lasting impression more powerful than an e-mailed résumé or brief cold call.

Job seekers should also keep their eyes and ears open regarding new community developments. Regularly check local news, whether online, TV, or print, to learn about new building construction. This might include announcements regarding new hospitals, restaurants, retail chains, or corporate headquarters. New construction means new jobs in building maintenance will soon be available, too.

CHAPTER FOUR

Best Foot Forward: The Interview Process

With the persistence, determination, and hard work needed to send out résumés and cover letters, pound the pavement, and network, you will likely reach the first goal of a job search: an interview with a prospective employer. Being asked to come in for an interview is a major accomplishment and a cause for celebration. Your work is not done, however. In some ways, it has only just begun.

Looking the Part

Building maintenance is considered a "blue collar" profession. Many maintenance jobs require clothing like uniforms or work shirts, jeans, boots, and other apparel that employees need for physical, and often dirty, working conditions. Job applicants need to look as professional as possible when interviewing, however, just like "white collar," or office workers.

Proper interview attire for men means a neat, pressed business suit, including jacket and slacks, formal shoes, a

A neat and professional appearance, confidence, friendliness, and other aspects of one's self-presentation will distinguish a job seeker during an interview. They will help the candidate win a position over others who do not convey as much professionalism and positivity.

button-down shirt, and a tie. Women should wear a skirt or pantsuit with a blouse, or a dress. When in doubt, always lean to the conservative. Avoid revealing or provocative clothing.

Tattoos and Piercings

While tattoos are more socially acceptable today than in years past, and perhaps more common in blue-collar industries and the trades, applicants should cover them up as best they can before an interview. Sober business attire should hide anything controversial. Similarly, remove or hide any unusual piercings and jewelry. Once a person gets a job, he or she should investigate employer policies regarding visible tattoos and piercings.

Dressing on a Budget

A teen or recent graduate might not have much money. Suits and business wear can be expensive, but that should not discourage young job seekers. They might find inexpensive clothing at area discount stores and outlets. By shopping well in advance of a job search or interview, young job seekers can take their time and hunt around for sales. This way, they won't have to feel pressured the week of an interview to find something appropriate at any cost.

Teens with tight budgets can try thrift stores such as Goodwill or Salvation Army outlets. Finding something that will fit properly will be more of a challenge, but not impossible, especially if a teen starts looking well ahead of the big day. Borrowing clothing from a parent, relative, or friend is also an option. A last resort might be to mix and match a respectable blazer with a pair of inexpensive but neat khakis.

E-mail and Phone Etiquette

Job hunters should make sure to check their e-mail at least once daily in case they receive responses to their job inquiries or applications. They should also check voicemails frequently and return calls promptly. Review all the instructions left by the employer in e-mails or voicemails and respond to them in a timely fashion.

If possible, write back the same day or the next day at the latest, and return calls as soon as possible, before the end of

If you receive a response to your application or résumé from a potential employer, be prompt in returning the call or e-mail. This will keep you at the front of the line for any available position. Remember the old saying: "You snooze, you lose!"

a workday or early the following one. Managers might receive dozens or even hundreds of responses for particular positions. Unless someone shows immediate interest after being contacted, employers will quickly move on to the next candidate on the list.

Knowledge Is Power

Good job candidates know both their skills and their limitations. Entry-level applicants will not need to know as much as older, experienced ones. However, knowing exactly how one's training and previous employment make an applicant right for the job is crucial. In the interview, candidates should be prepared to answer questions about their training in a way that demonstrates their skills and knowledge of the field. They should also ask questions of their own. In this way, they will demonstrate their curiosity about how things work in this particular facility and their awareness that they have more to learn and master and are eager and willing to do so.

Job candidates should make sure that their résumé lists any specific certifications (for example, in HVAC, boiler maintenance, electric, etc.) that they have earned. They should also emphasize these credentials during the interview. Each state has its own certification requirements and standards. While entry-level candidates can get jobs without certain certifications, any specialized skills or certifications will make their application stand out from the pack.

Usually, employers hire an entry-level worker with the understanding that he or she will achieve certain certifications in the future, while continuing to work for the building or company. Applicants should be aware of this and be prepared to agree to further training and education after they get their first job. This is especially true if they plan to move on to positions of greater responsibility, including managing large facilities and staffs.

Before the interview, applicants should learn as much as possible about the workplace they hope to be joining. The job listing will likely cover this information in some detail. An apartment building will demand different tasks than an industrial space, hospital, or school, for instance. Looking up an office building's tenants and exploring other public records that relate to the building may give teens an idea of what types of jobs might come up on any given day and what the typical duties would be. They can thus arm themselves with some useful talking points and intelligent, informed questions for the interview.

Final Preparations

The day of an interview can be an anxious one. Preparing ahead of time goes a long way toward reducing this tension. Things to consider when trying to make the day of the interview go as smoothly and calmly as possible include the commute, punctuality, and making sure you are in a good physical and mental state.

Contact Information

When setting up the interview, always ask for a contact number (both a landline and mobile number) for the person who will be interviewing you. Managers and other maintenance personnel are often away from their desks and may not be reachable at their landline. Provide your phone number to the interviewer, preferably a mobile. On the morning of the interview, make sure the mobile is fully charged and turned on. Appointments are sometimes cancelled by the interviewer at the last minute. And unexpected and unavoidable delays—like traffic jams or a delayed bus or train—might force you to call ahead to postpone.

In addition, request details about the interview location. It may not be in an office or an easily accessible room, but rather in an out-of-the-way part of a larger complex of buildings. Specific instructions will prevent job applicants from getting lost or confused, or entering a restricted area.

Planning the Commute

Job applicants should map out their commute as soon as they confirm the interview time and place. If there is any confusion, ask the contact person for exact details, including the street address; the nearest bus, train, or subway stops; and driving or walking directions. Never assume anything, and do not be embarrassed to ask. It is better to find out for sure and know exactly where you are going than to guess and end up in the wrong place at the wrong time.

Applicants should also carefully time their trip to the interview location according to their mode of transportation. An initial step is using an Internet mapping application like Google Maps or MapQuest. Figure out if the destination can be reached by public transportation, including trains, buses, or subways, or only by car or cab. If you drive, make sure you have enough gas and that the car is working properly. Standing

With the widespread availability of Internet-enabled devices, there are few excuses for sloppy planning when it comes to getting to an interview. Even if people lack Internet access, they should think ahead and ask a friend, relative, or other associate to help them plan their commute.

by your overheated or flat-tired car, miles from your destination, and calling at the last minute to cancel a job interview is a headache you don't need. Fairly or not, it will reflect poorly on you.

In the days before the interview, using whatever form of transportation you plan to take, do a trial run to the destination. Do it on a weekday, when traffic and ridership are at their peak, and at the time you will be doing it on the actual day of the interview. On the day itself, even if the Internet indicates that the interview site is only thirty minutes away and your dry run went flawlessly, give yourself at least an extra half hour or more. Traffic, breakdowns, and other problems can arise. Cutting things too close only adds unnecessarily to the anxiety before and during an interview. It is better to arrive twenty minutes early and have extra time to prepare and relax than be several minutes late, out of breath, sweaty, and totally stressed out.

At the Interview

Job applicants showing up at a workplace should introduce themselves to the receptionist, make it clear whom they are scheduled to see, and give the reason for their visit. They should follow instructions on where to wait and avoid unnecessary small talk. Receptionists or other employee are busy, so respect their time.

Meeting a prospective employer can be nerve wracking. Smile, offer a firm handshake, and be confident and relaxed. During the interview, answer questions in detail, knowledgeably, and in complete sentences. Try not to ramble on, offer unnecessary details, or exhibit nervous behavior. Avoid "pause words" and "conversation filler." These include words such as

Among other things, a handshake is a sign of confidence and respect. It is just one of many details for a job applicant to remember when conveying a sense of professionalism. Employers want to hire those who are eager, positive, and easy to get along with.

"um," "uh," and "like." They may strike an interviewer as anxious, unprepared, inarticulate, or unprofessional. Practice interviewing with a relative or friend beforehand to minimize this kind of awkwardness.

Other nervous activity includes excessive finger tapping, leg jiggling, biting one's fingernails, or playing with a pen or pencil, including doodling on paper. Applicants should give the interviewer their full attention, listen carefully to everything that is said, answer questions fully, and ask intelligent and informed questions.

Emphasize the positive and eliminate the negative. Bring up the positive aspects of your school and professional experiences, especially the practical knowledge you have acquired and the hands-on training you have received. Never complain

RECOMMENDATIONS AND REFERENCES

Teens should keep the contact information of trusted adults who are willing to recommend them for work or provide character references that employers use to make sure that job applicants are trustworthy and reliable. These contacts can include:

- Former employers: These can include anyone a teen has worked for, even if the job is unrelated to building maintenance, such as retail, restaurant, or other customer service—oriented work. Naturally, however, recommendations from skilled tradespeople whom a teen has worked under will have the greatest impact upon and relevance to employers.

- Teachers and instructors, especially shop teachers and technical and trade school instructors.

- Representatives or members of community groups, nonprofits, churches, and other organizations in which a teen may have volunteered his or her time and skills or assumed leadership roles.

about or criticize past teachers or bosses. No employer wants to hear a potential employee complain endlessly. It only makes them seem negative, disruptive, and undesirable as a potential hire.

Be honest about your work experience, skills, and training. Telling an interviewer everything he or she wants to hear, especially if it exaggerates your actual knowledge, abilities, and experience, will only get you into trouble and embarrassment in the near future. This is especially true in technical fields like building maintenance. A worker falsely claiming to know about certain machinery or procedures is bound to embarrass himself or herself sooner rather than later and get fired. Even worse, such dishonesty can endanger the worker, his or her coworkers, and the building's residents, tenants, or visitor. It can cause expensive and catastrophic damage to equipment or facilities.

Entry-level job applicants are not expected to know everything; that is why they are considered entry level. It is more important for interviewees to be presentable, energetic, enthusiastic, eager, and professional. Experienced professionals will often see right through false claims. If the candidate is not right for the job, both parties will be better off if the match does not work out. A candidate who honestly admits to his or her current limitations but expresses an eagerness and willingness to learn and grow will make a far better impression on the prospective employer.

After the Interview

Common professional courtesy demands that the interviewee send an e-mailed or written letter of thanks to anyone he or she met during the interview process. Candidates should thank everyone individually for their time and await their decision.

It can sometimes take a while to hear back, sometimes even a few weeks. Checking in once or twice during a long wait is acceptable, but applicants should avoid harassing the employer with constant requests for status updates. Some employers may call applicants back in for a second interview, and even a third, with different managers or superiors. A complicated and prolonged hiring process demands some patience from job seekers new to the field.

This young man is browsing job listings in the Brooklyn branch of the New York State Department of Labor Employment Services office. However difficult and discouraging it sometimes seems, staying positive and persistent are essential for job search success.

A job seeker might go on many interviews before getting hired. That is why it is important not to take rejection personally. In some cases, employers will simply not follow up with an applicant, while others may send a rejection letter or e-mail, depending on their policy.

Every interview, regardless of its end result, is a learning experience. Few applicants are lucky enough to be offered a job right away. It takes time, patience, and a willingness to keep searching for open positions, seeking leads from one's social network, and sending out countless résumés and cover letters. With persistence, one of these attempts will pan out. You'll ace the interview, and the next thing you know you'll be arriving on site for your first day of work.

CHAPTER FIVE

The New Guy: First Days on the Job

Getting that first job is quite an accomplishment, and the first day at work can be both anxious and exciting. The new employee's first duty is to watch, listen, and learn. This is the day when he or

Before your first day on the job, you should determine what the dress code is or if a uniform is required and how, when, and from whom you will obtain it.

she begins applying his or her education, training, and experience in an exciting new setting.

Starting Out: The New Hire Package

New employees should expect to take care of paperwork and other bureaucratic and administrative obligations during the first day or week on the job. Human resources staffers sometimes call this paperwork a new hire package.

Employers, especially corporations with large staffs, require new employees to receive company handbooks that outline policies and procedures. Many workplaces have standard consent forms for workers to sign. Examples include documents declaring that the worker realizes that his or her work e-mails and Internet activity may be tracked and that the employer has the right to administer drug tests to employees. Because building maintenance workers often handle heavy machinery and vehicles, they must agree to maintain a drug- and alcohol-free working environment. New hires are also informed about policies relating to sexual harassment and other inappropriate, unethical, or illegal behavior.

Health Insurance and Benefits

Employees with medical insurance and other benefits, such as pension or retirement plans, will usually receive explanatory materials and application forms related to these benefits. They are also given tax forms to fill out that determine how much local, state, and federal income taxes and Social Security taxes will be deducted from their paychecks. New employees

Before signing any paperwork, new hires should always review it carefully and make sure to ask supervisors about any details that concern them, no matter how minor they may seem. This helps prevent confusion or being taken advantage of later.

need to bring photo identification such as a driver's license and have their Social Security number handy for tax purposes.

New employees can ask their managers any questions they have about the paperwork. They are also encouraged to talk to their parents or other experienced, trusted working adults about these matters if they find them confusing. They need not make big decisions about benefit options on their first day. Instead, they should take the time to research and consider their options—such as level of health insurance or which retirement fund to invest in. They can then report back to human resources once they have made up their minds.

Making a Good Impression

It is important to make a good impression on the first day. This means arriving on time, preferably a bit early. Employers will provide uniforms or will have already informed new hires about the dress code. Employees may change into their clothes in a locker room on the job site, or they may be expected to show up dressed and ready to go. In either case, employees should arrive for work well rested and well groomed.

New hires will often be assigned a cubicle, workstation, or other work area. Keeping this area neat and orderly will make the workday run more smoothly and show supervisors and managers that the employee is organized and professional. A sloppy work area may also count against workers during periodic employment reviews.

Professional Behavior with Coworkers

Many people make friends at work, even lifelong ones. For newer members of the workforce, the camaraderie of the workplace can feel very much like the high school or college setting they are used to. However, workers must keep things professional, separating work responsibilities from socializing and friendship.

One area where workers need to stay professional is in their relationships with supervisors, managers, and other superiors, as well as with coworkers. Humor and horsing around might be necessary to relieve the occasional stress or tedium of work. But workers should avoid inappropriate

Modern workplaces, including blue-collar ones like those of building maintenance workers, have diverse staffs, including women. Avoiding offensive behavior and language is not only required due to workplace rules, but it is also the right thing to do.

language and humor related to race and ethnicity, religion, sexual orientation or sexuality, and other sensitive topics.

Many workplaces have policies discouraging or banning dating in the workplace, especially relationships between managers and their subordinates. Federal and state sexual harassment laws forbid employees in positions of power from dating lower-level workers. Workplace rules, often documented in an employee handbook or other literature, should give new hires an idea of what they can do if they feel harassed by a superior or coworker.

Professional Behavior with Clients, Tenants, and Residents

Workers can be friendly and even establish friendships with superiors and peers. However, it is a bad idea for employees to become too friendly with tenants, residents, students, or other "clients" who make use of the facilities where they work. Workers may say too much if they speak freely and risk offending clients or damaging the relationship between tenants and management.

Another danger is being tempted to do special favors "off the books" or "under the table" for particular people on a work site. Tenants may offer workers extra cash to fix something in their apartment, office, or work area that the tenant should be paying a professional to do. Similarly, a building tenant may quietly ask maintenance workers to do work off-site, at a private home or a place of business. All such offers and favors should be refused and avoided. Working off the books can get you fired if it is discovered. It also puts the employee at risk of getting in trouble with the Internal Revenue Service (IRS) for unpaid taxes.

A huge part of building maintenance is client satisfaction. A worker in this field needs to be a "people person." Politeness, cheerfulness, and a diplomatic ability to manage client needs are almost as important as technical skill. Any job has its fair share of deadlines, demands, difficulty, and stress. Building tenants or office workers may call about an emergency that needs to be fixed immediately. Some may be impatient, angry, or abusive. Building maintenance workers must keep calm

One benefit of working in building maintenance is the satisfaction one receives not simply from doing a good job, but also from the knowledge that one is helping others and making their daily lives just a little bit easier by ensuring that the building they live or work in operates as smoothly as possible.

and professional in such situations. Besides being unprofessional, arguing with or insulting clients is a surefire way to get a stern lecture from a manager. Too much of it could lead to a worker getting fired.

All in a Day's Work

Besides all the rules and relationships to become accustomed to during the first day, week, and month on the job, building maintenance workers usually begin learning the ropes almost

GOING GREEN

New workers in building maintenance are entering the job market during what some call the green building revolution. New government standards for energy-efficient and environmentally friendly building construction are changing the field. Workers can expect more automated systems and changes in building design and materials. Building maintenance technicians may soon be frontline troops in the effort to save more energy, resources, and money. As technology develops to meet this challenge, workers are in a unique position to learn these systems and to make sure that the facilities they work in are running as efficiently as possible. Hands-on participation in the green building revolution is one of the most exciting aspects of a building maintenance career.

immediately. They may work under, or "shadow," a more experienced colleague. Imagine being a new trainee shadowing a building maintenance technician in an office building, for example.

After getting to work, the building maintenance technician first checks e-mail and voicemail. Emergencies or unfinished tasks from a prior shift are the first priority, especially if something has come up overnight. One office manager has left a message about her office being too cold. The maintenance technician calls back, promising to stop by soon. After a few quick e-mail replies, the maintenance technician and the trainee check the central energy management system for any problems with that office's settings. Finding nothing wrong, they take measurements and call another technician, an HVAC specialist, to inspect the office's main heating unit. Returning to the office, the maintenance technician shows the new hire how to log the work order into the computer system.

Meanwhile, the maintenance department's computer system has generated an e-mail reminder that this is the week to change all the filters on the heating/cooling units in the building. Another technician arrives and shows the new employee how to calculate the number of filters needed. They visit the basement to retrieve the new filters. After being shown how to replace the old filters, the new hire is left to swap them out for new ones, a task that takes the rest of the morning.

After lunch, the new hire's manager guides the trainee through the central equipment management system, pointing out its electrical, plumbing, and HVAC functions. The manager also shows the trainee how to review and enter work orders, work the e-mail and voicemail systems, adjust lists of supplies, and go over receipts.

The new worker also meets some of the other staff, including another recent hire who is painting an empty office that is soon to be rented. Another is replacing a hallway door. The worker helps out with each task and finishes the day tired but eager to prove himself or herself the next day.

A Fulfilling Career

Building maintenance workers take pride in all the hard work and troubleshooting involved in making sure that a workplace or residence runs smoothly. Fixing problems for clients can be personally satisfying. Every day, building maintenance workers do the kind of work that their clients, tenants, and guests don't know how to or are unable to do for themselves.

Many workers also enjoy that they get to perform various tasks throughout their workday, rather than sitting in one place doing the same thing over and over again. As technology improves, workers also find themselves in an ever-changing workplace. They are constantly learning how to work with new tools, machines, and computer systems. Building maintenance jobs will continue to change. One thing that will not change is that the field itself will always provide its workers with exciting challenges, satisfying and rewarding work, and a feeling of tremendous pride and accomplishment.

accreditation Official recognition that a school or educational program meets certain government-mandated academic standards.

ATS Stands for application tracking system, a computer program used by employers that searches through résumés for keywords and other criteria.

blue collar Refers to jobs and careers in which people work with their hands, like the trades (plumbing, construction, welding, electrical, heating and cooling, etc.).

business casual A way of dressing professionally for work that is less formal than wearing a business suit. It usually involves slacks and a button-down or golf shirt for men, slacks or skirt and a blouse for women, and dress shoes for both sexes.

diploma mill Private technical school that provides unsatisfactory course work, instruction, faculty quality, and job placement for its paying students, and whose reputation among potential employers is very low.

embellish To exaggerate something, including adding false details to make one's story, background, or résumé more appealing.

FAFSA The Free Application for Federal Student Aid; this is an application for federal educational loans and grants.

green building Refers to new building construction and maintenance procedures that attempt to reduce energy use and waste.

HVAC Short for heating, ventilation, and air-conditioning, a specialized area of building maintenance.

hydronic Refers to a heating system that uses fluids, such as water, to deliver heat.

keyword Important word or phrase that can be entered into search engines to generate more specific and relevant results. Also the words that employers will be looking for in one's cover letter and résumé that indicate one's relevant academic or professional experience and qualifications.

mentor An experienced person who teaches someone a particular trade or discipline.

new hire package The collection of employment-related paperwork that many new workers receive.

off-the-books Also called "under the table," this refers to work done for cash, without reporting such income to government tax agencies.

shop class A high school–level course in which students learn metal- or woodworking.

super Short for "superintendent," a super is usually the sole building maintenance person in an apartment building.

termination Being fired from a job.

vocational Refers to education that prepares students for a particular job or career.

wear and tear The deterioration or damage that occurs from normal, longtime use of equipment.

white collar Refers to employees who work in professional or corporate and office settings.

Accrediting Commission of Career Schools and Colleges of
Technology (ACCSCT)
2101 Wilson Boulevard, Suite 302
Arlington, VA 22201
(703) 247-4212
Web site: http://oedb.org/accreditation-agencies/accsct
ACCSCT is dedicated to ensuring a quality education for
students who pursue career education at ACCSC-
accredited institutions. Its mission is to serve as a
reliable authority on educational quality and to promote
enhanced opportunities for students by establishing,
sustaining, and enforcing valid standards and practices
that contribute to the development of a highly trained
and competitive workforce through quality career-
oriented education.

American Society of Heating, Refrigeration, and
Air-Conditioning Engineers (ASHRAE)
1791 Tullie Circle NE
Atlanta, GA 30329
(404) 636-8400
Web site: http://www.ashrae.org
ASHRAE is an organization of workers specializing in HVAC
and related building technologies, with an emphasis on
sustainability and efficiency.

Building Service Contractors Association International
(BSCAI)
401 North Michigan Avenue, Suite 2200
Chicago, IL 60611

(800) 368-3414

Web site: http://www.bscai.org

BSCAI represents a worldwide network of more than one
thousand member companies that provide cleaning,
facility maintenance, security, landscaping, and other
related services to building owners and managers. The
association provides contractor-specific educational
programs, individual certifications, publications, a
members-only purchasing program, seminars, industry
data and research, and networking opportunities, all
developed specifically for leaders in the building service
contracting industry.

Human Resources and Skills Development Canada
(HRSDC)

Service Canada Enquiry Centre

Ottawa, ON K1A 0J9

Canada

(800) 563-5677

Web site: http://www.hrsdc.gc.ca

A division of the Canadian government, HRSDC is com-
mitted to career help for Canadian citizens. It provides
job assistance, career advice, and a number of other
services.

International Facility Management Association (IFMA)

1 East Greenway Plaza, Suite 1100

Houston, TX 77046-0194

(713) 623-4362

Web site: http://www.ifma.org

IFMA is an international trade organization that represents the interest of facility managers, provides accreditation, sponsors education, and conducts research on the field.

International Facility Management Association
British Columbia Chapter
1023 - 161A Street
Surrey, BC V4A 8G8
Canada
(778) 318-8844
Web site: http://www.ifmabc.org
The International Facility Management Association's Surrey chapter centers on the organization's activities in British Columbia, Canada.

Occupational Safety & Health Administration (OSHA)
200 Constitution Avenue NW
Washington, DC 20210
(800) 321-OSHA (6742)
Web site: http://www.osha.gov/youngworkers/index.html
OSHA assures safe and healthful working conditions for working men and women by setting and enforcing standards and by providing training, outreach, education, and assistance.

Service Employees International Union (SEIU)
1800 Massachusetts Avenue NW
Washington, DC 20036
(202) 730-7000

(800) 424-8592
Web site: http://www.seiu.org
SEIU is one of the largest labor unions, with members in
    building maintenance and services.

U.S. Department of Labor
Frances Perkins Building
200 Constitution Avenue NW
Washington, DC 20210
(866) 4-USA-DOL (487-2365)
Web site: http://www.dol.gov
The Department of Labor's mission is to foster, promote,
    and develop the welfare of the wage earners, job seek-
    ers, and retirees of the United States; improve working
    conditions; advance opportunities for profitable employ-
    ment; and assure work-related benefits and rights.

U.S. Equal Employment Opportunity Commission (EEOC)
131 M Street NE
Washington, DC 20507
(202) 663-4900
Web site: http://www.eeoc.gov
EEOC is responsible for enforcing federal laws that make it
    illegal to discriminate against a job applicant or an
    employee because of the person's race, color, religion,
    sex (including pregnancy), national origin, age (forty or
    older), disability, or genetic information. It is also illegal
    to discriminate against a person because the person
    complained about discrimination, filed a charge of dis-
    crimination, or participated in an employment

discrimination investigation or lawsuit. The laws apply to all types of work situations, including hiring, firing, promotions, harassment, training, wages, and benefits.

U.S. Green Building Council (USGBC)
2101 L Street NW, Suite 500
Washington, DC 20037
(202) 742-3792
(800) 795-1747
Web site: http://www.usgbc.org
USGBC is an organization promoting energy conservation in the construction and maintenance of buildings. It promotes the Leadership in Energy and Environmental Design (LEED) standard.

Web Sites

Due to the changing nature of Internet links, Rosen Publishing has developed an online list of Web sites related to the subject of this book. This site is updated regularly. Please use this link to access the list:

http://www.rosenlinks.com/JOBS/Build

Andrews, Brad. *Maintenance Technician: How to Land a Top-Paying Job*. Newstead, Queensland, Australia: Emereo Pty, Ltd., 2009.

Beco, Alice. *Cool Careers Without College for People Who Love Houses*. New York, NY: Rosen Publishing, 2007.

Callan, Mary Frances, and William J. Levinson. *Achieving Success for New and Aspiring Superintendents: A Practical Guide*. Thousand Oaks, CA: Corwin Press, 2010.

Carlson, Howard C., and John F. Eller. *So Now You're the Superintendent!* Thousand Oaks, CA: Corwin Press, 2008.

Chanter, Barrie, and Peter Swallow. *Building Maintenance Management*. Malden, MA: Wiley-Blackwell, 2007.

Crawford, Matthew B. *Shop Class as Soulcraft: An Inquiry into the Value of Work*. New York, NY: Penguin Books, 2010.

Doyle, Allison. *Internet Your Way to a New Job*. Cupertino, CA: Happy About, 2011.

Grensing-Prophal, Lin. *The Everything Résumé Book*. Avon, MA: Adams Media, 2012.

Harmon, Daniel E. *A Career as an Electrician*. New York, NY: Rosen Publishing, 2010.

Hill, Paul. *The Panic Free Job Search: Unleash the Power of the Web and Social Networking to Get Hired*. Pompton Plains, NJ: Career Press, 2012.

Levitt, Joel. *Facilities Management: Maintenance for Buildings and Facilities*. New York, NY: Momentum Press, 2012.

Levitt, Joel. *The Handbook of Maintenance Management*. New York, NY: Industrial Press, 2009.

Levitt, Joel. *Lean Maintenance*. New York, NY: Industrial Press, 2008.

Provenzano, Steve. *Blue Collar Résumés*. Independence, KY: Course Technology PTR/Cengage Learning, 2012.

Reeves, Ellen Gordon. *Can I Wear My Nose Ring to the Interview?: A Crash Course in Finding, Landing, and Keeping Your First Real Job*. New York, NY: Workman Publishing Company, 2009.

Stack, Carol, and Ruth Vedvik. *The Financial Aid Handbook: Getting the Education You Want for the Price You Can Afford*. Pompton Plains, NJ: Career Press, 2011.

Tomecek, Stephen M. *Tools and Machines* (Experimenting with Everyday Science). New York, NY: Chelsea House Publishing, 2010.

Wolny, Philip. *Money-Making Opportunities for Teens Who Are Handy*. New York, NY: Rosen Publishing, 2014.

Wood, Brian. *Building Maintenance*. Malden, MA: Wiley-Blackwell, 2009.

Atkin, Brian, and Adrian Brooks. *Total Facilities Management.* Oxford, England: Wiley-Blackwell, 2009.

Baltimore Business Journal. "How to Make the Résumé Stand Out." September 7, 2012. Retrieved September 20112 (http://www.bizjournals.com/baltimore/print-edition /2012/09/07/how-to-make-the-résumé-stand-out.html).

Booty, Frank, ed. *Facilities Management Handbook.* Burlington, MA: Butterworth-Heinemann, 2009.

Brown, Donn W. *Facility Maintenance: The Manager's Practical Guide and Handbook.* New York, NY: AMACOM, 1996.

Brown, Tara Tiger. "The Death of Shop Class and America's Skilled Workforce." Forbes.com, May 30, 2012. Retrieved August 2012 (http://www.forbes.com/sites/tarabrown /2012/05/30/the-death-of-shop-class-and-americas -high-skilled-workforce).

Burd, Stephen. "Texas Trade School Chain Faces Death Penalty Over Charges That It Cooked the Books on Job Placements." Higher Ed Watch/New America Foundation, August 3, 2011. Retrieved August 2012 (http:// higheredwatch.newamerica.net/node/55852).

Byrne, Matt. "Landlord Says Malden Building Superintendent Stole from Tenants." *Boston Globe,* August 16, 2012. Retrieved August 2012 (http://www.boston.com /yourtown/news/malden/2012/08/landlord_malden _building_super.html).

CareerOneStop. "Occupation Profile: Building and Grounds Cleaning and Maintenance." CareerInfornet.org. Retrieved September 2012 (http://www.careerinfonet .org/Occupations/select_occupation.aspx?next=occ _rep&level=&optstatus=&id=1&nodeid=2&soccode =&stfips=&jobfam=).

Community College of Allegheny County (PA). "Facilities Maintenance Technology." Retrieved August 2012 (http://www.ccac.edu/default.aspx?id=138620).

Cotts, David G., et al. *The Facility Management Handbook.* New York, NY: AMACOM, 2009.

Cruzan, Ryan. *Manager's Guide to Preventive Building Maintenance.* Danvers, MA: CRC Press, 2009.

Goodway Blog. "Latest Trends in Building and Facility Energy Efficiency." May 10, 2012. Retrieved July 2012 (http://www.goodway.com/hvac-blog/index.php/2012/05/latest-trends-in-building-and-facility-energy-efficiency).

Halligan, Ashley. "Today's Top 5 Careers in Facility Management." *Software Advice,* February 17, 2012. Retrieved July 2012 (http://blog.softwareadvice.com/articles/cafm/top-5-careers-in-facility-management-1021612).

Heck, Josh. "Wichita's Building Maintenance Companies Are Implementing Green Practices." *Wichita Business Journal,* November 29, 2009. Retrieved August 2012 (http://www.bizjournals.com/wichita/stories/2009/11/30/story5.html?page=all).

iSeek.org. "Building Maintenance Worker Interview." Retrieved August 2012 (http://www.iseek.org/industry/green/careers/building-maintenance-worker.html).

Lewis, Bernard T. *Facility Manager's Operation and Maintenance Handbook.* New York, NY: McGraw-Hill Professional, 1999.

Lewis, Bernard T., and Richard P. Payant. *The Facility Manager's Emergency Preparedness Handbook.* New York, NY: AMACOM, 2003.

Lewis, Bernard T., and Richard P. Payant. *Facility Manager's Maintenance Handbook.* New York, NY: McGraw-Hill Professional, 2007.

Magee, Gregory H. *Facilities Maintenance Management.*
Kingston, MA: R. S. Means Co., 1988.

Moore, Mary. "Building a Career in Facilities Management."
Boston Business Journal, June 15, 2012. Retrieved July 2012
(http://www.bizjournals.com/boston/print-edition/2012
/06/15/building-a-career-in-facilities.html?page=all).

PayScale.com. "Salary Stories: Building Maintenance Career."
December 14, 2009. Retrieved August 2012 (http://blogs
.payscale.com/salarystories/2009/12/salary-of-a-building
-maintenance-supervisor.html).

Pentland, William. "Green Building Sparks Battle for the Built
Environment." Forbes.com, September 2, 2012. Retrieved
September 2012. (http://www.forbes.com/sites
/williampentland/2012/09/02/green-building-sparks-battle
-for-the-built-environment).

U.S. Bureau of Labor Statistics. "General Maintenance and
Repair Workers." Retrieved August 2012 (http://www.bls
.gov/ooh/installation-maintenance-and-repair/general
-maintenance-and-repair-workers.htm).

Wordsworth, Paul. *Lee's Building Maintenance Management.*
Oxford, England: Wiley-Blackwell, 2001.

About the Author

Philip Wolny is a writer and editor from New York. He has written about high-risk construction work, moneymaking opportunities for handy teens, and other career-related topics. He fondly recalls tales of the building maintenance field from his father, a former contractor and onetime building maintenance technician and doorman.

Photo Credits